35 Song Hits
by Great Black Songwriters

Bert Williams, Eubie Blake, Ernest Hogan and Others

Edited by

David A. Jasen

DOVER PUBLICATIONS, INC.
Mineola, New York

DOVER MUSICAL ARCHIVES

All the selections in this volume are in the public domain in the United States. They may be used in these original versions or may be adapted or modified and used for any purpose, private, public, educational or commercial. No permission, fee or royalty payment is required. The above does not apply in countries outside of the United States where copyright protection may exist.

PUBLISHER'S NOTE

Since the originals reproduced here are faithful historical documents as well as sources of enjoyment, the titles and artwork have not been changed even where they reflect the broader humor of their era, in which the nation was far less sensitive to jibes about minority groups. It is our belief that a mature understanding of our past is more fruitful than a falsification of history.

Copyright

Copyright © 1998 by Dover Publications, Inc.
All rights reserved under Pan American and International Copyright Conventions.

Published in Canada by General Publishing Company, Ltd., 30 Lesmill Road, Don Mills, Toronto, Ontario.
Published in the United Kingdom by Constable and Company, Ltd., 3 The Lanchesters, 162–164 Fulham Palace Road, London W6 9ER.

Bibliographical Note

35 Song Hits by Great Black Songwriters: Bert Williams, Eubie Blake, Ernest Hogan and Others is a new collection of music, with original covers, selected and with an introduction by David A. Jasen, first published by Dover Publications, Inc., in 1998. Names of composers, lyricists, and original publishers appear in the list of contents and on the individual covers and title pages.

International Standard Book Number: 0-486-40416-1

Manufactured in the United States of America
Dover Publications, Inc., 31 East 2nd Street, Mineola, N.Y. 11501

INTRODUCTION

This unique collection celebrates the great contributions of African-American composers and lyricists during the earliest decades of Tin Pan Alley's existence, from 1878 to 1922. In addition to the work of superb Alleymen like Chris Smith, James Reese Europe, and Clarence and Spencer Williams—who created some of the most important pop songs of all time—this folio contains highlights from the history of black Broadway shows. Here are the great tunes of such composers and lyricists as Ernest Hogan, Alex Rogers, James Weldon Johnson, Noble Sissle and Eubie Blake—and, especially, Bert Williams, the greatest comedian of the young century. Although Williams (with partner George Walker) hired the foremost black songwriters of the day to supply songs for their shows, Williams himself—a star performer—found time to write some seventy published songs—more than most full-time show composers. A fair sampling of his best work is part of the thirty-five memorable songs in our edition.

The traditionally short Broadway runs of black shows had little effect on their popularity as productions toured the country, sometimes for several years, giving added life to their songs; some black writers—both in and out of touring show productions—struck it lucky. Joe Jordan scored heavily when Fannie Brice sang "Lovie Joe" in the 1910 *Follies*, and Dabney and Mack's "That's Why They Call Me Shine" lived on to become a standard in the Dixieland band repertoire. Shelton Brooks' "Some of These Days" took on legendary life as Sophie Tucker's theme song, and James Bland's "Carry Me Back to Old Virginny" was elevated to official song of the state of Virginia.

With the deaths of Walker, Hogan, and of the gifted Bob Cole—forever linked in black theater history to brothers J. Rosamond Johnson and James Weldon Johnson (an outstanding poet of this century)—black shows disappeared from Broadway from 1911 until the birth of Sissle and Blake's *Shuffle Along* in 1921. That historic production renewed public interest, starting a trend toward black shows that lasted the entire decade of the 1920s. *Shuffle Along* alone, with its lovely ballad "Love Will Find a Way" and hugely popular "I'm Just Wild About Harry," enjoyed 484 performances on Broadway and toured the country for two years with *three* national companies!

These funny, sweet, melancholy, toe-tapping tunes remain a cornerstone of popular American music of the early century. Our edition honors the contributions of the remarkable black composers, lyricists, musicians and performers who brought them to us all.

David A. Jasen

Contents

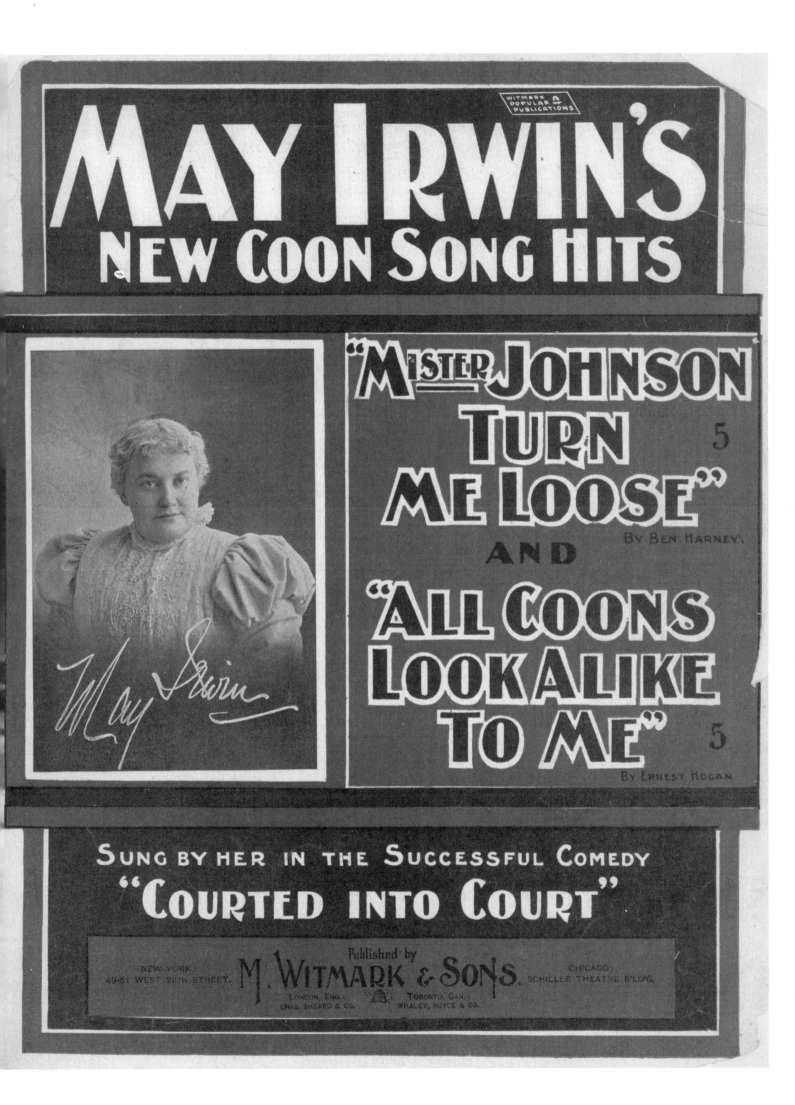

All Coons Look Alike To Me.

Words and Music by ERNEST HOGAN.

f

(vamp till ready)

1. Talk a-bout a coon a hav-ing trou-ble, I
2. Nev - er said a word to hurt her feel-ings, I

think I have e - nough of ma own, Its all a - bout ma Lu-cy Jane-y Stubbles, And
always bou't her presents by the score, And now my brain with sorrow am a reel- ing, Cause

she has caused my heart to mourn, Thar's an-oth-er coon bar-ber from Vir-gin-ia, In so-
she won't accept them any more, If I treat-ed her wrong she may have loved me, Like

ci-'ty he's the leader of the day, And now ma hon-ey gal is gwine to quit me, Yes she s
all the rest she's gone and let me down, If I'm luck-y I'm a gwine to catch my pol-i-cy, And

Recite.

gone and drove this coon a-way, . . She'd no ex-cuse, . . To turn me loose, I've been a-
win my sweet thing way from town, For I'm wor-ried, . . Yes, I'm des-p'rate, I've been Jo-

-bused, . . I'm all con-fused, . . Cause these words she did say. . . .
-nahed, . . And I'll get dang'rous, If these words she says to me. . . .

All coons look a - like to me, I've got an-oth-er beau, you see,

And he's just as good to me as you, nig! ev - er tried to be,

He spends his mon - ey free, I know we cant a-gree, So

1. I don't like you no how, All coons look a-like to me, **2.** me.

All coons look a - like to me, I've got an-oth-er beau, you see,

And he's just as good to me as you, nig! ev - er tried to be,

He spends his mon - ey free, I know we cant a-gree, So

I don't like you no how, All coons look a-like to me, me. *8va.*

BIG SONG HITS

FROM THE

DARKTOWN FOLLIES

IN
A THREE ACT MUSICAL COMEDY
ENTITLED
"MY FRIEND FROM KENTUCKY"

BOOK, LYRICS,
MUSIC AND STAGING BY
J. LEUBRIE HILL

NIGHT TIME	60¢
DEAR OLD DIXIE	60¢
WAITING ALL DAY LONG	60¢
LOU, MY LOU	60¢
YOU	60¢
ROCK ME IN THE CRADLE OF LOVE	60¢
THAT'S THE KIND OF MAN I WANT	60¢
GOOD TIME WHILE I CAN	60¢
THE MAN OF THE HOUR	60¢
★ AT THE BALL THAT'S ALL	60¢

LAFAYETTE PUBLISHING CO.
LAFAYETTE THEATRE   NEW YORK N.Y.

EDITED BY EDGAR LEVEY

At The Ball, That's All

Words and Music by
J. LEUBRIE HILL

My! but that mu - sic sounds so sweet I just can't keep still __ up -
Clouds of joy float - ing 'round the hall __ A reign __ of hap - pi - ness

on my feet, __ 'Cause __ rag - time mu - sic to me __ is a per - fect
seems to fall, __ It is so en - tranc - ing while danc - ing at a rag - time

treat: (Spoken) (Because it certainly can't be beat) When at a ball you are feel - ing kind - er
ball: (Because it makes a hit with all) When at a ball __ and you feel some-what

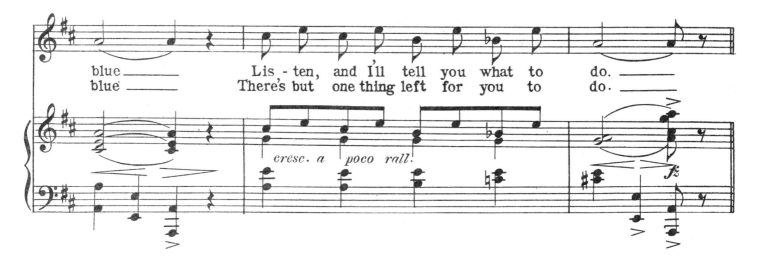

blue __ Lis - ten, and I'll tell you what to do. __
blue __ There's but one thing left for you to do. __

cresc. a poco rall.

Just work your shoulder, Snap your fingers one and all, In the hall at the ball that's

all. _____ all. _____

DANCE

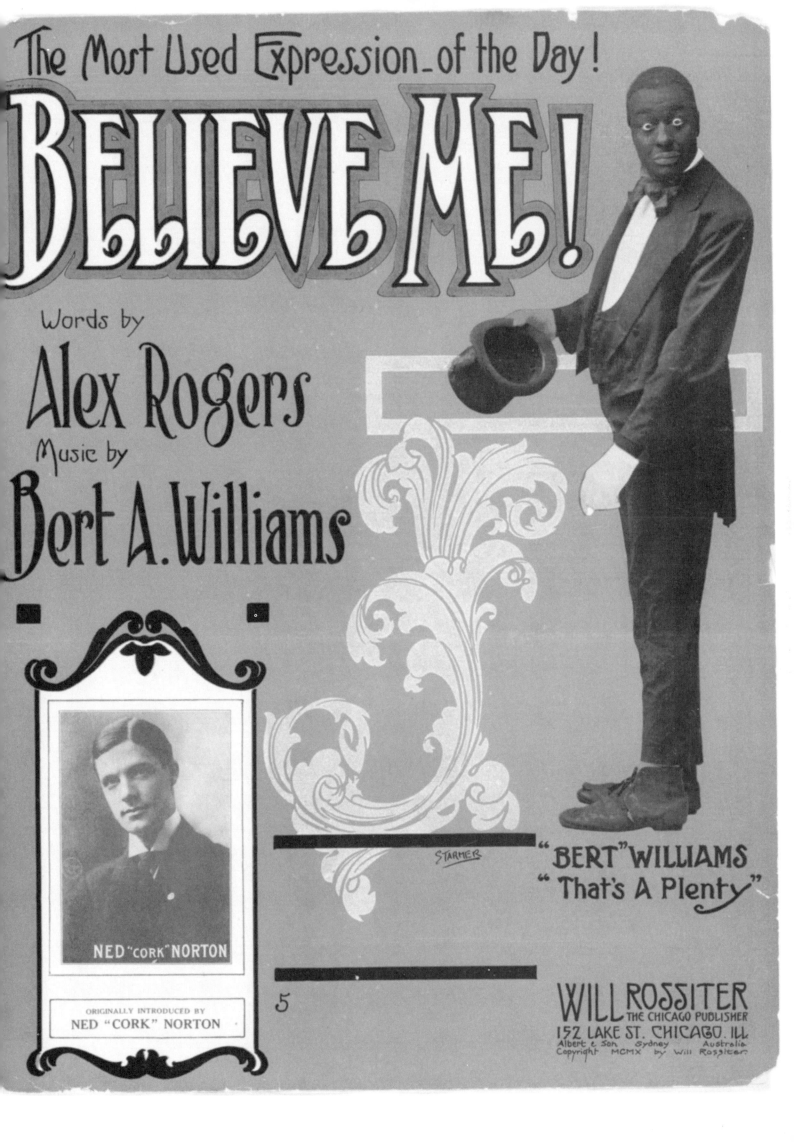

BELIEVE ME.

Words by ALEX ROGERS.

Music by BERT A. WILLIAMS.

Copyright, MCMIX, by Will Rossiter, Chicago, Ill.

12

Brother-'N-Law Dan

By JOE JORDAN

Lov - ie Joe you all know
Look here, Dan un - der-stand

Was loved by all the girls for miles a - round Jen - nie Pearl
I ain't ac - cu-sin' you of do - in' wrong But I'm 'fraid

was his girl They mar - ried, took a flat and set-tled down
you done played This lov - in' rack - et just a lit - tle strong

16

Joe's brother Dan came to vis - it one day   Jen - nie she fell dead in love with
I came home this _ morn - in' 'fore day   Start - ed in as us - ual with my

him right a - way   She said "I'm sure it's lone - some for you
par - rot to play   Now Dan, I ain't sus - pis - cious but I'm

down in Ten - nes - see   Won't you come and live with us and
blamed if I can see   What my pol - ly meant by screech - in'

keep me com - pa - ny,   You know,   I   know: ____
out these words to me,   Like this   and   this: ____

CHORUS

Broth-er'n-law Dan   Broth-er'n-law Dan   You can love much bet-ter than your

broth - er Joe can___   You've got a lov-in' whis__per that just

tick - les my ear,   And a tan-ta-liz-in' voice that I just

loves to hear___   And when you are a-way from me I   raves and raves I

TWO PLANTATION MELODIES! STANDARD AND POPULAR!

CARRY ME BACK TO OLD VIRGINNY.

SONG AND CHORUS. WORDS AND MUSIC BY JAMES A. BLAND. 40.

THERE'S A HAPPY LITTLE HOME.

SONG AND CHORUS. WORDS AND MUSIC BY HARRY WOODSON. 40.

BOSTON:

OLIVER DITSON COMPANY.

NEW YORK: CHICAGO: PHILADELPHIA: BOSTON:

CHAS. H. DITSON & CO.,   LYON & HEALY,   J. E. DITSON & CO.   JOHN C. HAYNES & CO.

CARRY ME BACK TO OLD VIRGINNY.

SONG AND CHORUS.

Words and Music by

JAMES BLAND.

Author of "The Old Homestead," "In the morning by the bright light," &c., &c.

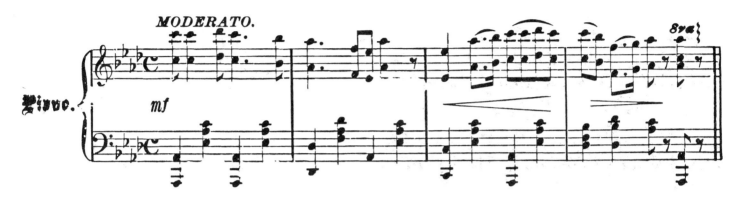

1. Car - ry me back to old Vir - gin - ny, There's where the cot - ton and the
2. Car - ry me back to old Vir - gin - ny, There let me live 'till I

corn and ta - toes grow, There's where the birds war - ble sweet in the spring-time,
with - er and de - cay, Long by the old Dis - mal Swamp have I wandered,

There's where the old dar - ke'ys heart am long'd to go,   There's where I labored so
There's where this old dar - ke'ys life will pass a - way.   Mas - sa and mis - sis have

hard   for   old mas - sa,   Day af - ter day   in   the   field of   yel - low corn,
long gone before me,   Soon we will meet   on   that bright and gold - en shore,

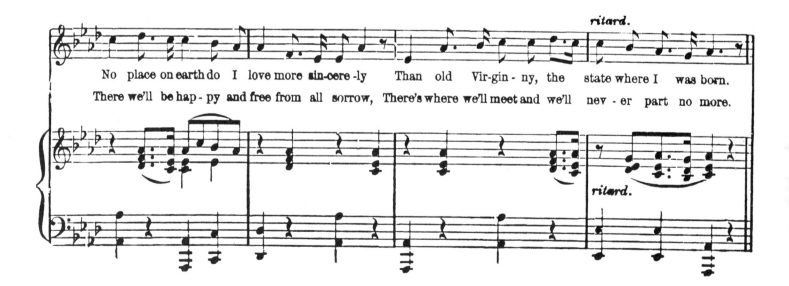

No   place on earth do I love more sin - cere - ly   Than   old Vir - gin - ny, the   state where I   was born.
There we'll be hap - py and free from all   sorrow,   There's where we'll meet and we'll   nev - er   part no more.

CHORUS.

Car-ry me back to old Vir-gin-ny, There's where the cotton and the corn and tatoes grow,

Car-ry me back to old Vir-gin-ny, There's where the cotton and the corn and tatoes grow,

ritard. Repeat pp last time.

There's where the birds warble sweet in the spring-time, There's where this old darkey's heart am long'd to go.

There's where the birds warble sweet in the spring-time, There's where this old darkey's heart am long'd to go.

ritard.

ritard.

"Come After Breakfast"

(Bring 'Long Your Lunch And Leave 'Fore Supper Time.)

by
BRYMN, SMITH and BURRIS.

Chorus. *(slow)*

Come af-ter breakfast, bring 'long your lunch and leave 'fore sup-per time. ___ If

you do that ___ I'm pos-i-tive ___ that I will treat you fine; For

ev'-ry body's wel-come at my house whe-ther in ___ rain or shine, If they

come af-ter breakfast bring 'long their lunch and leave 'fore supper time. ___ time.

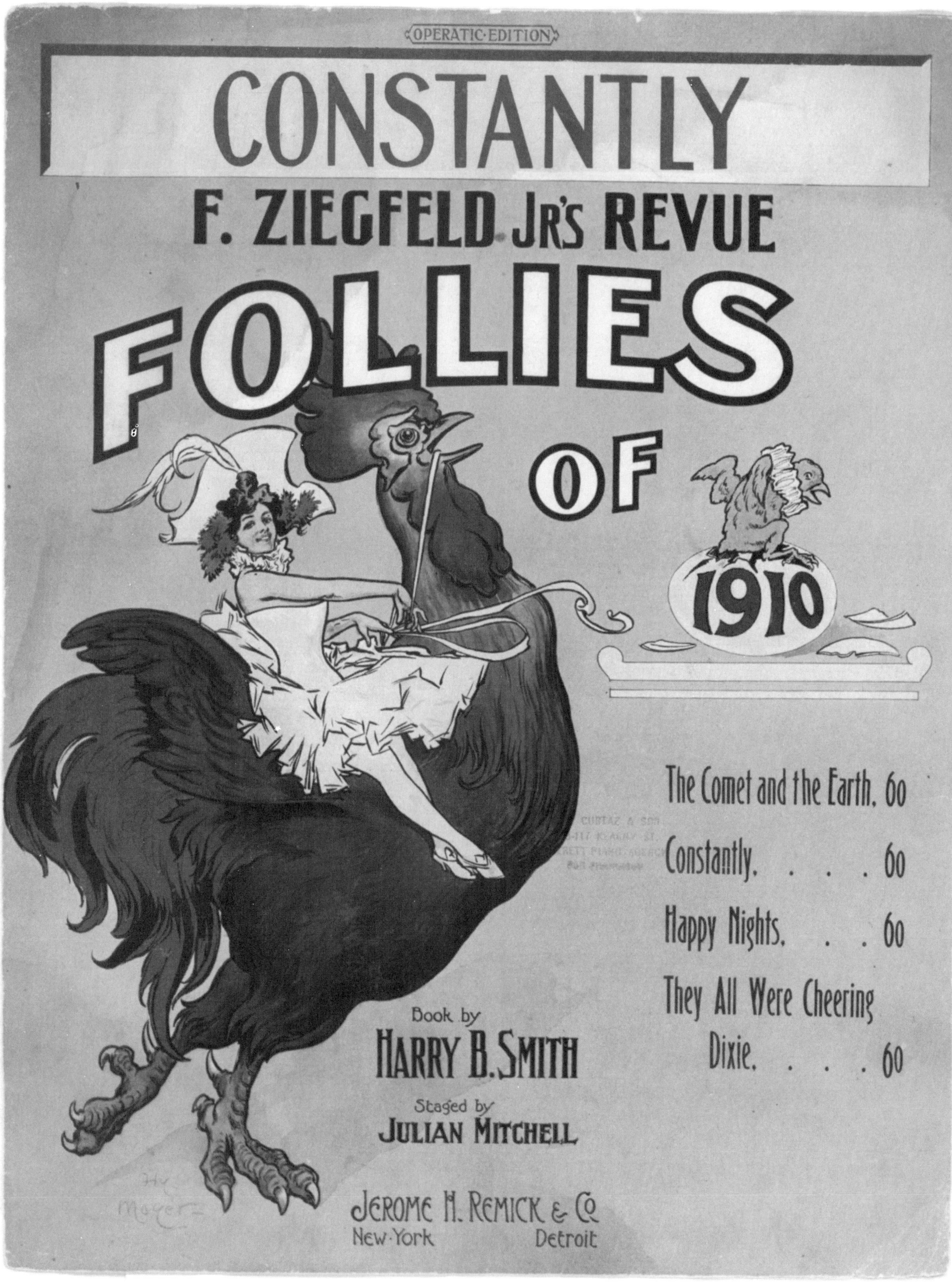
OPERATIC EDITION
CONSTANTLY
F. ZIEGFELD JR'S REVUE
FOLLIES
OF
1910
The Comet and the Earth. 60
Constantly. . . . 60
Happy Nights. . . 60
They All Were Cheering
Dixie. . . . 60
Book by
HARRY B. SMITH
Staged by
JULIAN MITCHELL
Hy Mayer
JEROME H. REMICK & Co
New York Detroit

Constantly

Words by
SMITH and BURRIS

Music by
BERT WILLIAMS

I used to be a luck - y moke A - spend - ing mon - ey
As a prize fight-er once I thought I'd try, I fought a man they

was a joke, But now it seems dat I stay broke con - stant - ly._____ I
called Kid Nye, Dat man he sho' did find my eye con - stant - ly._____ I

CHORUS

Good luck wans me, dorns me, scorns me, con - stant - ly, _____

Bad luck meets me, seeks me, greets me, con - stant - ly, _____ Some

times I feel like a bird in a tree, Fly-in' round so__ gai-ly and free, But it

seems, hard luck clips my wings for me con - - stant - ly.

THE GREATEST COON SONG EVER WRITTEN!

DORA DEAN

"The Sweetest Gal You Ever Seen"

CLIFFORD & HUTH.

Words and Music

BY

Williams

AND

Walker

SCHOTTISCHE

Arranged by

GEO. W. HETZEL.

Sung

With Great Success

BY

Clifford

AND

Huth

AND MANY OTHERS

SONG

4

Piano Solo, 40.   Band, 50.   Orchestra, 10 Parts, 60.   Orchestra, 14 Parts, 80.   Piano Accompaniment, 15.   First Violin Part, 10.

PUBLISHED BY

BRODER AND SCHLAM

39 WEST 28 STREET, NEW YORK.   26, 28, 30, O'FARRELL STREET, SAN FRANCISCO, CAL.

CHARLES SHEARD & Co. 192 HIGH HOLBORN, LONDON ENG.)

DORA DEAN.

Arranged by
GEO. W. HETZEL.

Words and Music by
BERT. A. WILLIAMS.

1. Way down in Lou - 'si - an - a, Dat's where ole Sis - ter Han- nah,
2. While down with Sis -ter Hol - ley, We all did feel so jol - ly,

Bakes the crack - lin bread up - on the coals.............; With her daughter Do - ra Dean, Who
Each one tried to cut a pig - eon wing... ....; When up jump'd Do '- ra Dean, Who

is my dear - est queen, Oh! I tell you, boys, she is a lump of gold.................. She
said I am the queen, I can beat you in a dance for an - y-thing.................. That just

goes to church on Sun - day, You'll find her home on Mon - day,
suit - ed ole Aunt Di - nah, Who sang a tune in mi - nor,

Help - ing all the folks the house to clean..............; Their home it looks so neat, You'll
Think - ing that she could the mu - sic make...............; So we start - ed in to test, To

find it hard to beat, The way its kept by Do - ra Dean...........
see who was the best, And Do - ra walk'd off with the cake.............

CHORUS.

Oh! have you ev - er seen my Do - ra Dean, She is the

p and *ff*

sweetest gal you ev - er seen; I'm gwine to make this gal sweet Do - ra,

queen, Next Sun - day morn' I'm gwine to mar-ry sweet Do - ra Dean........ Dean...........

D. C.

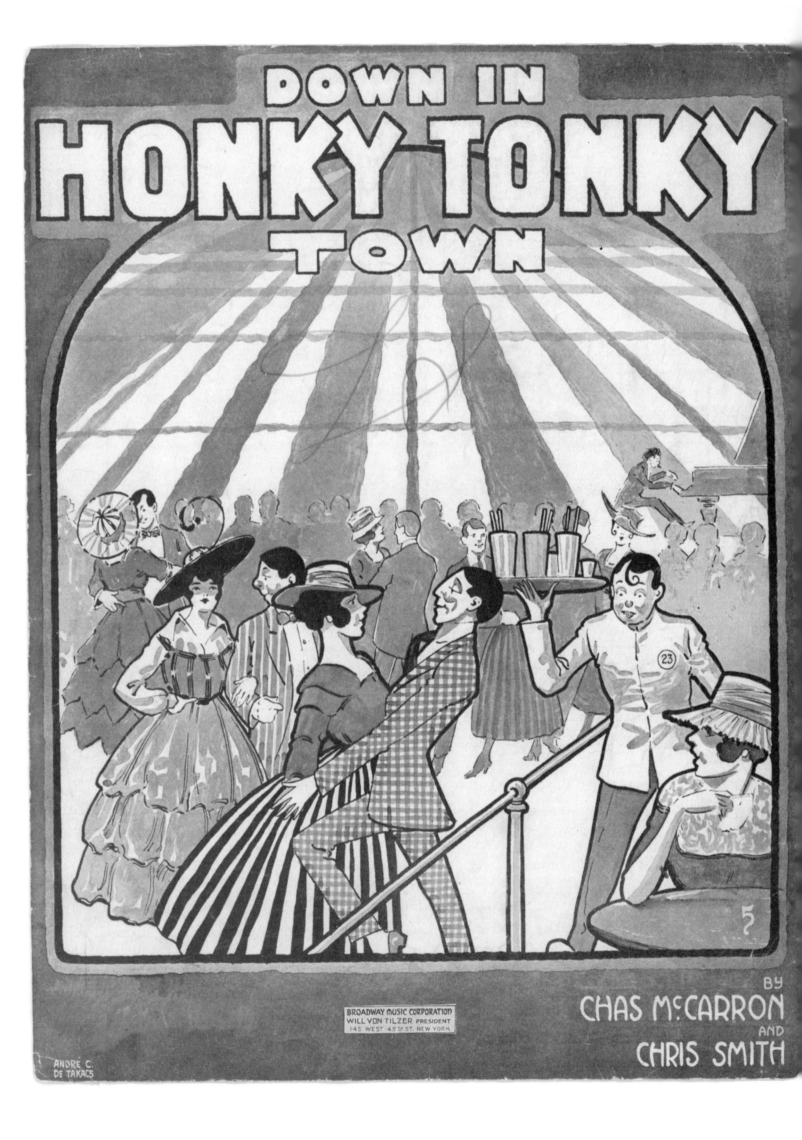

DOWN IN HONKY TONKY TOWN

By CHAS McCARRON
and CHRIS SMITH

Moderato

VOICE

Vamp till ready

Bill Johnson said one day, To his E - li - za May, We've been to
That Hu - la Hu - la dance, Don't e - ven stand a chance, You ought to

near - ly ev - 'ry place in Town ___ If you sug - gest to me some oth - er nov - el - ty,
see those lit - tle dus - ky queens ___ They do the "Bom - ba shay," they do it in a way,

We both will go and do the thing up brown ___ His sweet - ie said, "My dear" there is a
You real - ly think you're back in New Or - leans ___ It's got to be a fad, With ev - 'ry

place I hear, I got it straight from Mose who brings the clothes, Its Hon - ky Ton - ky Town,
gal and lad, To go to Hon - ky Ton - ky Town at night, Each girl - ie cries to go,

37

SELECTIONS FROM
WILLIAMS & WALKER'S
MUSICAL COMEDY SUCCESS

Bandana Land

DIRECTION
F. RAY COMSTOCK

BOOK & LYRICS BY
J. A. SHIPP
AND
ALEX ROGERS

MUSIC BY
WILL MARION COOK

INTERPOLATIONS BY
BERT A. WILLIAMS

THE
GOTHAM-ATTUCKS
MUSIC COMPANY
AND
THE HOUSE OF MELODY

Fas', Fas' World.

Chorus.

'Tis a fas' world,— one mo' fas,' fas' world,— De
'Tis a fas' world,— one mo' fas,' fas' world,— He
'Tis a fas' world,— one mo' fas,' fas' world,— Dat

man what says,— "Oh, I'll git mine,—
did-'nt have noth-in' when he went in,—
night was hot,— but here's a fact,—

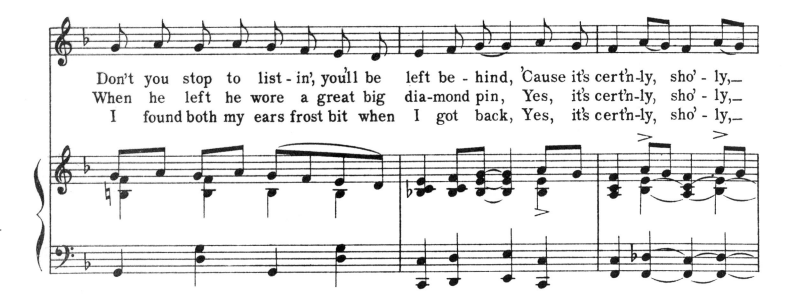

Don't you stop to list-in', you'll be left be-hind, 'Cause it's cert'n-ly, sho'-ly,—
When he left he wore a great big dia-mond pin, Yes, it's cert'n-ly, sho'-ly,—
I found both my ears frost bit when I got back, Yes, it's cert'n-ly, sho'-ly,—

42   *Fas', Fas' World*

tru - ly,   pos - i - tive - ly,   one   mo'   fas',   fas'   world. ___
tru - ly,   pos - i - tive - ly,   one   mo'   fas',   fas'   world. ___
tru - ly,   pos - i - tive - ly,   one   mo'   fas',   fas'   world. ___

IV.

I met a po' boy on the street, just a few days ago,
   He said, he was jes eight years old, and looked as if 'twas so,
He said, "I am an orphan, Pa died in the Civil War,
   Give me a quarter to help my Ma, she died right after Pa?"

Chorus.

Tis a fas', fas' world, one mo' fas,' fas' world,
   That kid worked on my feelings so,
I clean forgot that war was thirty years ago,
   Gee this is cert'nly, sho'ly, truly, pos'tively, one mo' fas' fas' world.

V.

I saw six kids jump on one boy, in a side street one day,
   I stopped and asked them why they all bear one boy in that way,
The bigges' boy of them said to me, "Now, "Cull," jes take your time,
   This kid's be shining shoes for five, the UNION price is a dime.

Chorus.

Yis a fas', fas' world, one mo' fas', fas' world,
   The police came and made a grab,
The UNION, they all "beat it" but they got the scab,
   My this is cert'nly, sho'ly, truly, pos'tively, one mo' fas', fas' world.

VI.

I heard an undertaker talking to his friend one day,
   I'm going to move away next week, the living here don't pay,
There's just one doctor in this town and that won't do for me,
   Now, up in Greenwille, where I'll move the towns got twenty-three.

Chorus.

It's a fas', fas' world, one mo' fas,' fas' world,
   He sure was a master of his trade,
He's figured out the death rate twenty years ahead,
   Deed this is cert'nly, sho'ly, truly, pos'tively, one mo' fas,' fas' world.

A Good Man Is Hard To Find

By EDDIE GREEN

My heart's sad and I am all for-lorn,— My man's treat-ing me mean,—
Yes-ter-day my heart from care was free,— I sang all_ through the day,—

I re-gret the day that I was born, And that man of mine I've ev-er seen,— My
Now the Blues have o-ver-ta-ken me, Since my lov-in' man has gone a-way,— I

hap-pi-ness it nev-er lasts a day,— My heart is al-most break-ing while I say:____ A good
tried my best to treat him nice and kind,— But now these words are run-ning thro' my mind:____ A good

Chorus

man____ is hard to find,_____ You al-ways get____ the oth-er kind,_____ Just

when you think that he is your pal.__ You look for him and find him fool - ing 'round some oth - er gal, Then you rave,_____ you ev - en crave_____ To see him lay - - ing in his grave;_____ So if your man is nice take my ad - vice and hug him in the morn - ing Kiss him ev - 'ry night,__ Give him plen - ty lov - in', treat him right__ For a good man now a - days is hard to find._____ A good find._____

GOOD MORNING CARRIE!

Words by R. C. McPHERSON.

Music by SMITH & BOWMAN.

Moderato.

1. In sun-ny South Car-'li-na lives an old aunt Di-nah And her daughter named Car-o-
2. There's dusk-y suit-ers plen-ty that would take my Car-rie from me, But she's promised to be on-ly

line. She's winsome cute and air-y, her folks they call her Car-rie, I hope some day, that she'll be
mine. With ten-der songs of woo-ing like the tur-tle dove a coo-ing, They ser-en-ade my Car-o-

mine. To meet her ev - 'ry ev - 'ning when the stars are bright-ly beam-ing Brings
line. We'll be wed - ded soon thats cer - tain and some hearts will be a hurt - in' When

joy and pleas-ure to my heart so lone, In the light of ear - ly dawn with my
budding leaves and flow - ers tell 'tis spring, There'll be no great dis - play but

ban - jo on my arm, I a - wake her from her slum - ber with this song:
on our wed - ding day, We'll ask the folks a - round to kind - ly sing:

mf

poco rit.

THE NEW MUSICAL SHOW

Mr. Lode of Koal

BOOK & LYRICS BY
J. A. SHIPP and ALEX ROGERS
ENSEMBLES BY ROSAMOND JOHNSON
SONGS BY BERT. A. WILLIAMS

Selling Agent
WILL ROSSITER
THE CHICAGO PUBLISHER
152 LAKE ST. CHICAGO. ILL.
Albert & Son Sydney Australia
Copyright MCMIX by Will Rossiter

STARMER

The Harbor Of Lost Dreams

Words by ALEX ROGERS

Music by BERT. A. WILLIAMS
Arr. by J. Rosamond Johnson

Copyright, 1909, by Will Rossiter, Chicago, Ill. British Copyright Secured

live for years And the ones where pre - cious jew - els rare You
shïn-ing goal The ones where thro' rose scent - ed air You

gave un - to your la - dy fair For these and all I
ride up to your cas - tle where De - part - ed friends and

think that there Must be a rest - ing place some wher̈e Oh there
sweet- hearts fair All anx - i - ous - ly a - wait you there

CHORUS

must be a har - bor of dreams some - where In that yon - der land way

I Ain't Gonna Give Nobody None O' This Jellyroll

Words and Music by
SPENCER WILLIAMS and
CLARENCE WILLIAMS
"You're Some Pretty Doll"
"You Can Have It, I Don't Want It"
"You're So Cute"

Wil - lie Green from New Or - leans a greed-y boy was he For he al - ways want-ed a
Wil - lie Green was real-ly mean and ver - y stin - gy too, He al-ways want - ed some of

lot a kids, Just to keep his com-pan - y, One day his ma bought him a jel - ly roll The
what you had But he gave noth-ing to you, And when his ma would give him jel - ly roll To

best cake that was made And when the kids be-gan to hang a - round Lit - tle Wil-lie said. I
hide it he would try And when the kids would ask him for a bite You'd hear Wil-lie cry.

Copyright 1919 by Williams & Piron, Music Publishers, New Orleans, La.

ERNEST HOGAN
THE UNBLEACHED AMERICAN

THE
In THE NEW SPECTACULAR SONG COMEDY
OYSTER MAN

MUSIC BY
WILLIAM H. VODERY & ERNEST HOG[AN]

DIRECTION OF
HURTIG & SEAMON

STORY BY
HAL RIED

LYRICS BY
HENRY S. CREAMER

ADDITIONAL
LYRICS BY
LESTER WALTON

Theatrical and Music Hall Rights of this Song are
Reserved. For Permission apply to the Publishers.

M. WITMARK & SONS
NEW YORK   CHICAGO   LONDON   PARIS
JOSEF WEINBERGER, LEIPZIG AND VIENNA
ALLAN & CO. MELBOURNE, AUSTRALIA
CANADIAN-AMERICAN MUSIC CO LTD. TORONTO

I Can't Keep My Eyes Off Of You.

Words by
LESTER A. WALTON.

Music by
WILL H. VODERS
& ERNEST HOGAN.

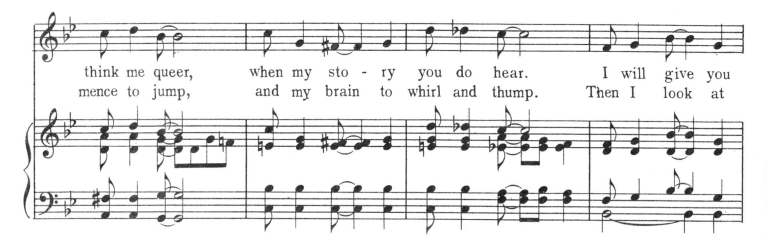

think me queer, when my sto - ry you do hear. I will give you
mence to jump, and my brain to whirl and thump. Then I look at

my ex - cuse___ for act - in' such a sil - ly goose, But
you and gaze,___ like a small child___ in a maze, Now

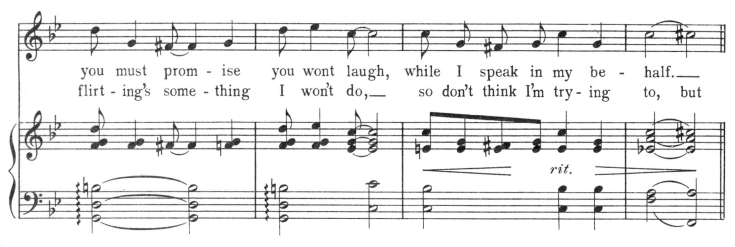

you must prom - ise you wont laugh, while I speak in my be - half.___
flirt - ing's some - thing I won't do,___ so don't think I'm try - ing to, but

rit.

CHORUS. *Slowly.*

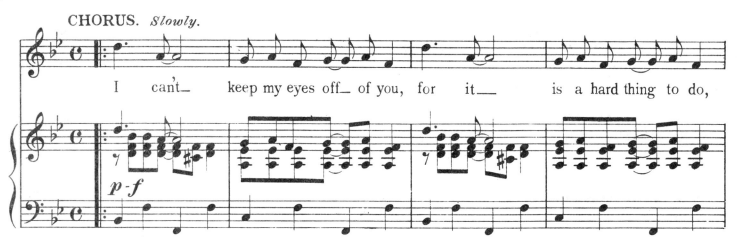

I cant___ keep my eyes off___ of you, for it___ is a hard thing to do,

p - f

I May be Crazy, But I ain't no Fool.

Words & Music by ALEX ROGERS.

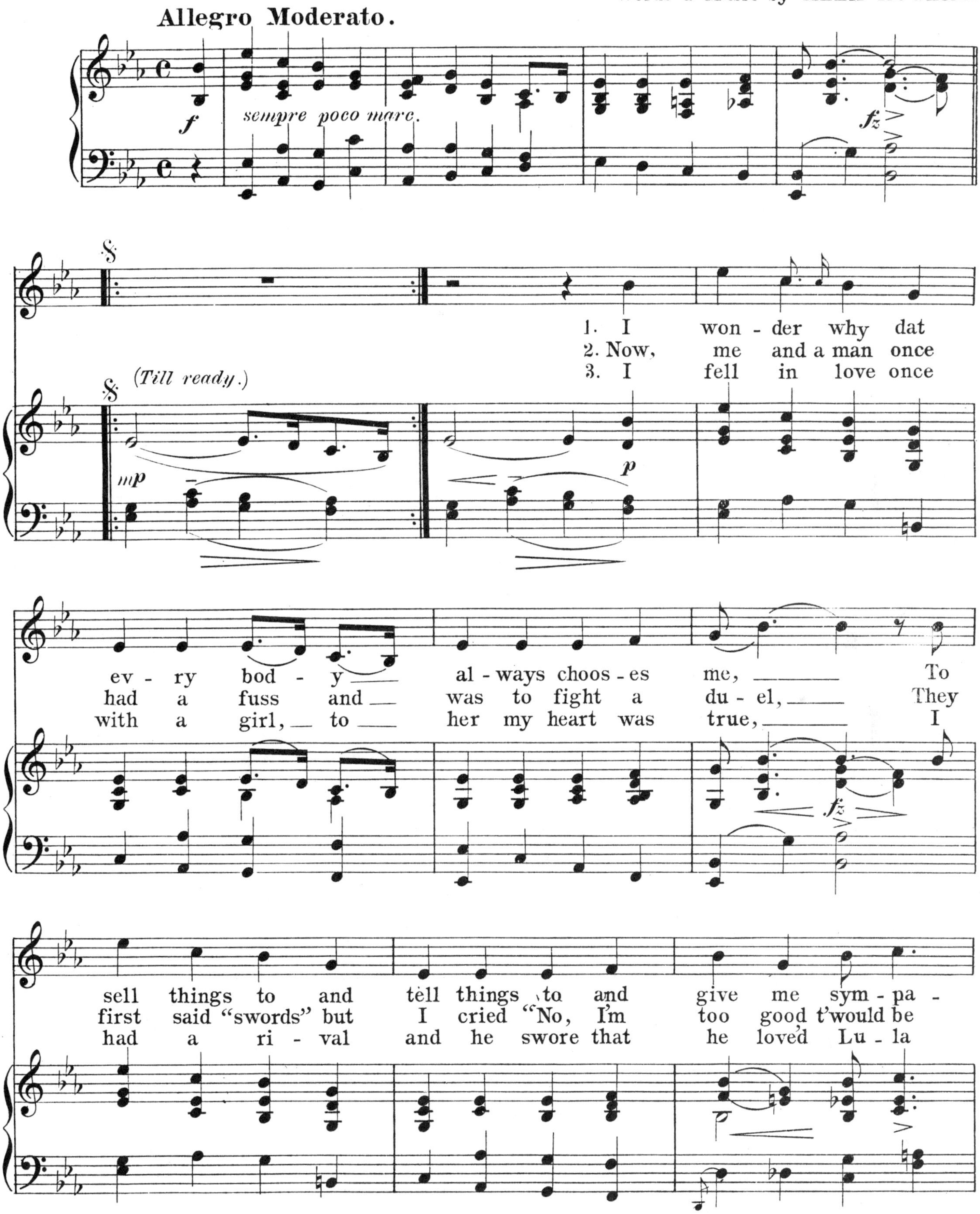

I'm goin' to Live anyhow, till I die.

Words & Music by
SHEPARD N. EDMONDS.

Allegro moderato.

1. Now there's a
2. When he'd de -

coon down 'n Tennessee, __ Who is as quaint as he can be; __ He nev-er
cid - ed to re - form, __ He started off to church one morn; __ And he was

b'lieves in 'ten din' church, nor goin' to Sun - day school; So all the
togged up in his best and out on good - ness bent; He thought he'd

peo-ple for him prayed, And all the good things 'bout him said; But he be-
be a real good coon, And be a Black-ville Dea-con soon; But much to

lieved in su - per - sti-tion as a rule. _____ He be-
his sur-prise they had an ac-ci - dent. _____ You see the

lieved in so-cial strife and hav'n a good time all his life, And to
choir refused to sing, Be-cause the church-bell wouldn't ring, Then this

be so wicked   he seemed not a - fraid; _____ They knew he
coon be-came sus - pic-ious and a - fraid; _____ He says "the

couldn't live ve-ry long   So when they asked him to re - form,   He near-ly
good folks I can't see   If dat's re - ligion ex - cuse me",   And as he

broke dat con - gre - ga-tion when he   said. _____
left, these are the words they heard him   say. _____

CHORUS.

I'm goin' to live an - y - how till I   die, _____   I

knows ma'kind of a life aint ver-y high: _____ With
2ᵈ time. Now

sticks and stones a you can break a ma bones, You may
it's a fact and it is of - ten said, That

talk all you want to 'bout me when I'm gone, But
when you die you are a long time dead,

I'm goin' to live an- y - how till I die. _____

I'M JUST WILD ABOUT HARRY
(HARRY)

SHUFFLE ALONG, Inc. Presents
THE NEW YORK MUSICAL NOVELTY SUCCESS

Shuffle Along

Book by
Flournoy
Miller
and
Aubrey
Lyle

Lyrics & Music by
Noble
Sissle
and
Eubie
Blake

Baltimore Buzz	60
Bandana Days	60
Daddy Won't You Please Come Home	60
Everything Reminds Me of You	60
Gypsy Blues	60
Good Night, Angeline	60
Honeysuckle Time	60
I'm Just Wild About Harry	60
If You've Never Been Vamped By a Brown Skin	60
I'm Craving for That Kind of Love	60
I'm Just Simply Full of Jazz	60
Kentucky Sue	60
Love Will Find a Way	60
Liza Quit Vamping Me	60
Low Down Blues	60
Old Black Joe and Uncle Tom	60
Oriental Blues	60
Pickaninny Shoes	60
Shuffle Along	60
Vision Girl	60

M. Witmark & Sons
New York

OPERATIC EDITION

Printed in U. S. A.

I'm Just Wild About Harry

ONE STEP SONG

Words & Music by
NOBLE SISSLE
& EUBIE BLAKE

There's just one fel - low for me in this world ___
There are some fel - lows that like all the girls, ___

Har - ry's his name ___ That's what I claim ___ Why
I mean the vamps, ___ With cru - el lamps, ___ But

I'M LIVIN' EASY.

AS SUNG BY

Lew Dockstader,
Lottie Gilson,
Barnes and Sisson,
Belle Davis,
Montgomery & Stone,
Williams & Walker,
Emma Carus,
Merri Osborne,
Irene Franklin,
Dolly Mestayer,
Clarice Vance,
Johnson and Dean,
The Eldridges,
Gertie Gilson,
The Brownings,
Ernest Hogan,
Steve Jennings,
The Davenports,
Edwin R. Lang,
Three Mortons,
Maud MacIntyre,
Gus Pixley,
Frank Cushman,
Four Luciers,
Carl Anderson,
Wilson & Massoney,
Lydia Hall,
Ida Howell,
and
Jones, Grant & Jones

WORDS & MUSIC
BY
IRVING JONES
COMPOSER OF
"GET YOUR MONEY'S WORTH" ETC.

F.A.Mills
MUSIC PUBLISHER
NEW YORK
48 WEST 29TH STREET.
CHICAGO.
CENTRAL MUSIC HALL BUILD'G
COR. STATE & RANDOLPH STS.

5

I'M LIVIN' EASY.

by IRVING JONES.

Composer of
{
Get Your Money's Worth.
Let Me Bring My Clothes Back Home.
If They'd Only Fought With Razors In The War.
Every-body Have A Good Time.
Gimme Back Dem Clothes.
}

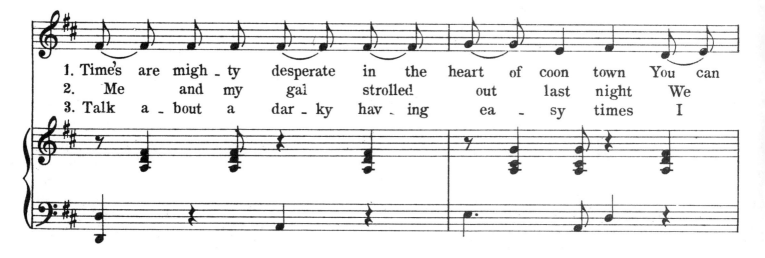

1. Time's are migh _ ty desperate in the heart of coon town You can
2. Me and my gal strolled out last night We
3. Talk a _ bout a dar _ ky hav _ ing ea _ sy times I

hard _ ly find a fat and health _ y coon a _ round, But
had _ n't gone far un _ til we got in _ to a fight, A
eat the best of food and drink the best of wines, And

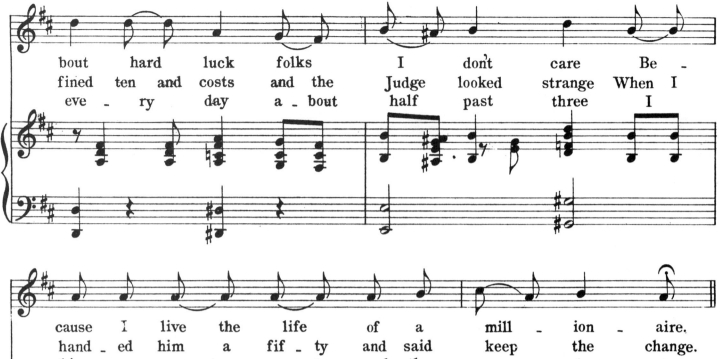

bout hard luck folks I don't care Be -
fined ten and costs and the Judge looked care strange When I
eve - ry day a - bout half past three When I

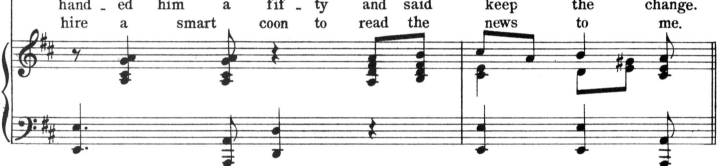

cause I live the life of a mill - ion - aire.
hand - ed him a fif - ty and said keep the change.
hire a smart coon to read the news to me.

CHORUS.

I'm liv - in' ea - - sy _____ eat - in' pork chops

grea - - zy, _____ al - ways got mon - ey

_to give my hon - - ey,_____ I'm al - ways

pick - - in'_____ on a spring chick - - en,_____

Yes, I am liv - in' ea - sy and cert'n - ly liv - in'

1.
high._____ I'm liv - in' high. 2. high._____

I Never Knew

(I Could Love Anybody Like I'm Loving You.)

Society Fox Trot

Revised by
PAUL WHITEMAN

By TOM PITTS, RAY EGAN
and ROY K. MARSH

Moderato

I al-ways thought ___
I used to smile ___

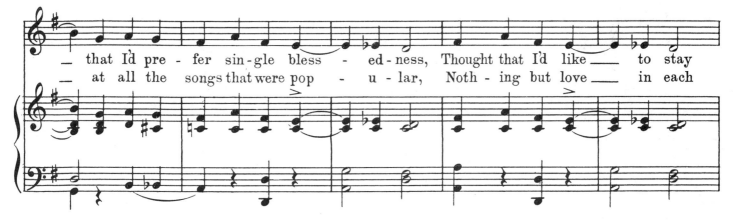

___ that I'd pre-fer sin-gle bless - ed-ness, Thought that I'd like ___ to stay
___ at all the songs that were pop - u - lar, Noth-ing but love ___ in each

free, ___ I nev-er thought ___ my time would come to mar - ry,
song, ___ I used to think ___ those kind of songs were fool - ish,

No wed-ding bells — for me. — I've changed my mind — af - ter
Now I ad - mit — I'm wrong. — Love songs are part — of my

all, — You are the one — made me fall; For
plan, — Show me the Min - is - ter man; For

rall.

CHORUS (*Slowly*)

I nev - er knew I could love an - y - bod - y, Hon-ey, like I'm

p-f

lov - ing you; — I could-n't re - al - ize — what a

pair of eyes   And a ba-by smile could   do;_____

I can't sleep,   I can't eat,   I nev-er knew a sin-gle soul could

be so sweet,_____   I nev-er knew I could   love an-y-bod - y,

Hon-ey, like I'm lov - ing   you.   you._____

EVERYBODY'S HAPPY

Gems

from the Musical Production

RUFUS RASTUS

ERNEST HOGAN

Direction of
HURTIG & SEAMON

5

PUBLISHED BY
CHAS·K·HARRIS
NEW YORK
CHICAGO
CANADIAN-AMERICAN MUSIC CO. LTD·TORONTO·CANADA.
ALBERT & SON
LONDON AND SYDNEY

After The Ball

STARMER

Is Everybody Happy?

Words by
FRANK WILLIAMS.

Music by
ERNEST HOGAN and
TOM LEMONIER.

85

Den Miss Eve she took a bite Ad - am eat the rest all right dats
P. T. Bar-num bought de Show Noah ___ could-n't make it go, he

why dey say the deb - ble is a Vil - lian.___
whet home on de ear - ly morn - ing train.___

CHORUS.

Is ev - 'ry bod - y hap - py?___ Is

ev - 'ry bod - y glad?___ Want ev - ry one a

laugh-in',_____ Don't want an-y—bod-y sad,_____

Want to see yo'sides a shak-in',_____ Laugh an' roll roun' on de

floor._____ Get hap-py, hap-py, hap-py,_____ Whoop'em

up an' laugh some more._____ more.

LIKIN' AIN'T LIKE LOVIN'.

Words and Music by
JAMES REESE EUROPE.

CHORUS

I may like (Lin - dy, I may like Joe_____
Lar - ry

May flirt with (Cin - dy And flirt with Flo;_____
Har - ry In fun you know;_____

(Tess-ie and Bess-ie, I may like too,_____ But
Ted-dy and Fred-die,

Lik-in' ain't_ like lov-in' love_ and I love you._____ you._____ *D.S.*

92 *Likin' Ain't Like Lovin'*

Alta S. Carleton

LOVE WILL FIND A WAY

SONGS WRITTEN – SUNG AND FEATURED
BY THE WELL KNOWN WRITERS AND ENTERTAINERS

NOBLE Sissle and EUBIE Blake

POPULAR 60 STANDARD PICTORIAL

M. WITMARK & SONS
NEW YORK

Love Will Find A Way

Words and Music by
NOBLE SISSLE
and
EUBIE BLAKE

Come, dear, and don't let our faith weak-en, Let's keep our love fires burn-ing bright Your love for me is heav-en-ly bea-con, Guid-ing me through love's dark-est night. Don't start mind-ing

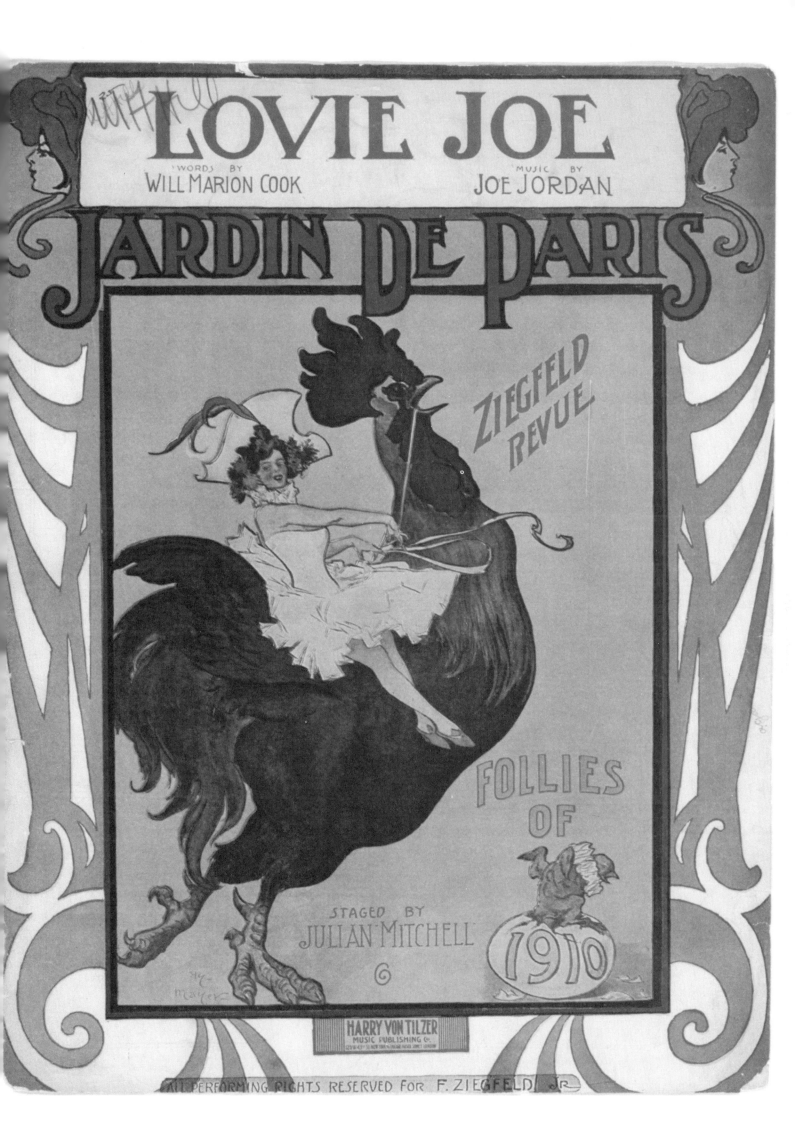

LOVIE JOE.

Words by
WILL MARION COOK

Music by
JOE JORDAN

Moderato

sad,............ I'm glad,............ I'm mad............ A -
py............ that's me,............ you see,............ I'm

bout that lov - in' man o' mine, He's............ so neat............ an'
feel - in' like a coo - in' dove, Say!............ the way............ that

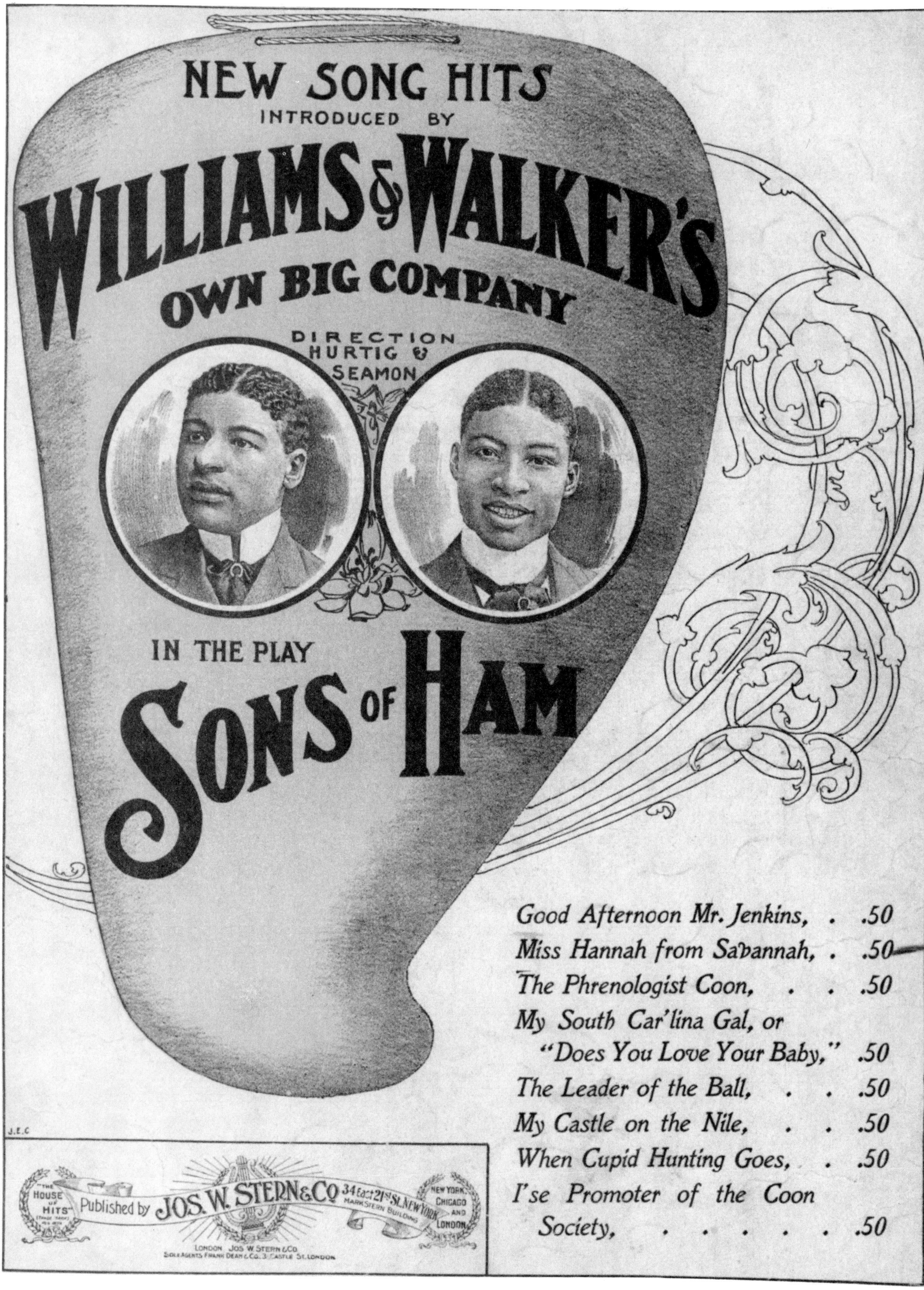
NEW SONG HITS
INTRODUCED BY
WILLIAMS & WALKER'S
OWN BIG COMPANY
DIRECTION HURTIG & SEAMON
IN THE PLAY
SONS OF HAM
Good Afternoon Mr. Jenkins, . .50
Miss Hannah from Savannah, . .50
The Phrenologist Coon, . . .50
My South Car'lina Gal, or "Does You Love Your Baby," .50
The Leader of the Ball, . . .50
My Castle on the Nile, . . .50
When Cupid Hunting Goes, . .50
I'se Promoter of the Coon Society, ...50
Published by JOS. W. STERN & CO. 34 East 21st St. NEW YORK
NEW YORK, CHICAGO AND LONDON
LONDON JOS. W. STERN & CO.
SOLE AGENTS FRANK DEAN & CO. 3 CASTLE ST. LONDON

MISS HANNAH FROM SAVANNAH.

Words by R. C. Mc PHERSON.

Music by THOS. LEMONIER.

Up from the land of the
They said I must be - -

fra - grant pine, Came a dus - ky maid - en to this
more cul - tured, Be - fo' mah stand - in here could

North-ern clime; She told all her friends, Ah's gwine to see The
be as - sured; That ah need - neb - er spec to be A

dif-f'rence in the sas - si - e - ty, __ Ah's heard so much 'bout their
fig-ure in their sas - si - e - ty, __ Why dere's none ob dem wid ma

high - toned way, 'Bout dem act - in' more like white folks
ped - i - gree, There's needer root nor branch to deir

ev' - ry day, If dey tries to come it on
fam - i - ly tree, If dey eb - - er fo'ce me

me too gran', Ah'll tell 'em who I am. __
to de wall, I'se gwine to tell dem all. __

poco rall.

colla voce.

CHORUS.

My name's Miss Han-nah, from Sa - va - an - nah,   Ah

wants all   you folks to un - der - sta - and - ah;

Ahm some   de blue-blood ob de la - and - ah,   I'se Miss Hannah from Sa _

va - an - nah!   nah! _____

NOBODY

Bert William's
Latest Oddity
successor to
"I MAY BE CRAZY
BUT I AIN'T NO FOOL"

Words by
ALEX ROGERS
Music by
BERT A. WILLIAMS

5

CROWN MUSIC CO.
SOLE SELLING AGENTS
12 East 17th Street, New York

"NOBODY."

Words by
ALEX ROGERS.

Music by
BERT A. WILLIAMS.

soothes my thump-ing, bump-ing brain? (Nobody! When
says "Come in and have a beer?" *Spoken.* (Nobody! I
says "Look at that hand-some man?" (Nobody! When

win-ter comes with snow and sleet, And me with hun-ger and cold feet, Who
had a steak some time a-go, With sauce I sprink-led it all—Oh! Who
all day long things go a-miss, And I go home to find some bliss, Who

says "Here's two-bits, go and eat?"— (Nobody!
said "That sauce is Ta-bas-co?"—*Spoken.* (Nobody!
hands to me a glow-ing kiss?— (Nobody!

Chorus. *SLOWLY.*

I _____ ain't nev-er done noth-in' to no - - bod-y;

I _____ ain't nev-er got noth-in' from no - bod - y, no time:

And _____ un-til I get some-thin' from some - bod - y, some-time, I

don't _____ in-tend to do noth-in' for no - bod-y _____ no_ time _____

Nobody 109

NOBODY.

A man and wife they fought one day,
I interfered in a friendly way,
Who said "don't have a thing to say?" *Nobody.*
The man he knocked off all my chin,
The woman kicked my ribs all in,
Who cried out "Shame! my what a sin?" *Nobody.*

When I fussed with Bill Jones 'bout Mame,
And I called Bill out of his name,
Who said I'd never look the same? *My Grandma.*
When Jackson threw a brick one day,
And my face it was in the way,
Who was it had the most to say? *Dr. Smith.*

Last fall when things were looking bright,
I started to whittle a stick one night,
Who cried out "Stop! that's dynamite?" *Nobody.*
When I in swimming went one day,
And on the banks my clothes did lay,
Who took my clothes far, far away? *Somebody.*

I donned a bathing suit one morn,
The only one I'd ever worn,
Who told me that the pants were torn? *Nobody.*
When I at one time wrote a play,
And played the play upon Broadway,
Who said go off and drive a dray? *Alan Dale.*

When I on ship for London bound,
Was many, many miles from ground,
Who helped me keep my dinner down? *Nobody.*
The time I had that foolish fit,
And struck a guy with this small mitt,
Who told me it was Hackenschmidt? *Nobody.*

When I was with my brother Claude,
And met a mule which kicked and pawd,
Who told me that her name was Maud? *Nobody.*
When I was slammed against a tree,
And Maud "Hee-hawed" with deviltry,
Who dug the horse-shoes out of me? *Nobody.*

When I fell off the Flat-iron block,
With force enough to stop my clock,
Who spread a net to stop the shock? *Nobody.*
When I was in that railroad wreck
And thought I'd cashed in my last check,
Who took the engine off my neck? *Nobody.*

On The Road To Monterey.

Words and Music
by BOB COLE.

Andante.

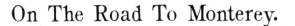

Piano.

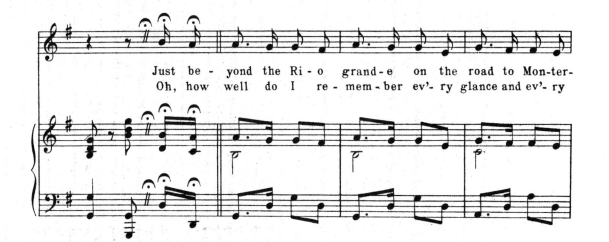

Just be - yond the Ri - o grand - e on the road to Mon-ter-
Oh, how well do I re - mem - ber ev'- ry glance and ev'- ry

ay, Near a beaut-i-ful la-goon-a where the birds sing night and
smile, How my heart is kept a-bump-ing and a-thump-ing all the

day; I be-held a pret-ty maid-en with a pair of rogu-ish
while, When that pret-ty Sen-o-ri-ta gave to me a tin-y

eyes, That en-chant-ed me like star-light in the skies.____
kiss, How it filled my soul with such ecs-the-tic bliss.____

____ When I asked the pret-ty maid-en would she hop in-to my
____ Still I thought I would for-get her yet it seems I ne-ver

Rastus Johnson, U.S.A.

Lyric by
ALEX ROGERS.

Music by
BERT A. WILLIAMS.

won some coin___ some time a-go___ in the Lou-is-an-___a
Lon-don I___ just thought I'd take___ a run to dear___ old

Lot - ter - y___ I bought five - hun - dred suits of clothes and
Pa - ris, gay___ To buy more wine___ and see more, sights and

went the world to see The first place that___ I
throw more, coin___ a - way But tell you all___ the

land - ed was in Lon - don, o'er the way where I
truth, Folks, Pa - ris ain't no hit with me cause

changed, my clothes so much they called me "Light - ning Ras - tus J,"
all, you get___ on ev' - ry hand is "Wee Mon - sieur Wee Wee" A

"Save It For Me!"

Words by
JAS. W. JOHNSON.

Music by
BOB COLE.

court Miss Ma-til-da Lee; Ev' - ry night,_____ to
just for a "tee-ny" part; If _____ with me, _____ a

tell her his love he'd try, All_____ he
lit-tle **you** will di - vide, I _____ will

did,_____ was to stam-mer these words and sigh:_____
try_____ my best to be sat - is - fied._____

rall.

Some of these days

Words & Music by
SHELTON BROOKS.

Arr. by Will Dorsey.

- Till ready -

Two lov-ers had been goin' to-geth-er
This lit-tle girl-ie felt so bad she

for some-time they lived down in a coun-try town,_____
thought that she would pack her things and go a - way,_____

When he told the girl-ie he was goin' a-way_____ her
But her lit-tle beau he quick-ly heard the news_____ and

lit - tle heart just melt - ed down._____ She
then he came back home next day._____ But

said, you know I love you hon - ey best of all____ so
when he reached the house he found that she had gone____ to the

please dont go a - way,_____ just as he went to go
de - pot he ran with vim,_____ The train it was pul - ling out

it grieved the girl - ie so these words he heard her say.
he heard his girl - ie shout these words she sang to him.

Chorus.

Some of these days_____ you'll miss me hon - ey_____

Some of these days_____ you'll feel so lone - ly_____

you'll miss my hug - ing_____ you'll miss my kiss - ing_____

you'll miss me hon - ey____ when you go a - way_____ I feel so

lone - ly_____ just for you on - ly_____ for you know hon - ey_____

you've al - ways had your way_____ and when you leave me_____

I know it will grieve me_____ you'll miss your lit - tle ba - by_____

yes some of these days._____ some of these days._____

Take Your Time.

EXTRA VERSES BY TOM BROWN.

I.

A friend of mine dropped in one day, as I sat down to dine,
  I said, "sit down and have a bite, you are a pal of mine,"
He said he wasn't hungry, but before he got through,
  I had to say, "Hold on old pal, this meal wa'n't cooked for you!"

Chorus.

Take your time, not so fast, take your time you won't last,
  For your appetite cert'nly is fine,
Every time your lip drops, then you grab for some chops,
  Take your time, this one's mine, take your time."

II.

I furnished up a flat on the installment plan,
  To furnish paying up the bill, it seems I never can,
My wife just buys up all the junk, that happens her way,
  Rugs, and clocks and pictures, if the men would only say,

Chorus.

Take your time, dear lady, take your time it's easy,
  And the cheapest and best way you'll find,
For a fourteen dollar bed, you pay thirty-five instead,
  Take your time, graft is fine, take your time.

III.

I had a toothache once so bad, I thought I would die,
  So at the painless dentistry, I thought I'd take a try,
The doctor threw me in the chair, I started to shake,
  But when he closed down on my tooth, I cried; "For goodness sake,

Chorus.

Take your time, doctor please, take your time, give me ease,
  Let the blamed old tooth ache, I don't mind,
For to tell you the truth, you've my jaw, and not my tooth,
  Take your time, this face is mine, take you time.

IV.

My brother Bill was slow of speech, and stammered quite bad
  He got a job, at school to teach, through some good friends he had,
There came a boy, Bill did'nt know, he stammered you see,
  It made Bill sore, he said, "Here b-b-boy, are you making f-f-fun of m-m-me."

Chorus.

T-t-take your time I'm no joke, t-t-take your time, silly moke,
  It's the best thing to do you will find,
There's some more I would say, that I can't say to-day,
  Ain't g-g-got time, never mind, t-t-take your time!

Take Your Time.

Words by
HARRISON STEWART.

Music by
JOE JORDAN.

mine, _____ When folks rush up _____ to you and say _____ what they
day, _____ She said I was _____ the fin - est man _____ that she

want you to do, _____ Just think it o - ver be -
ev - er had seen, _____ But when she tal - ked a - bout

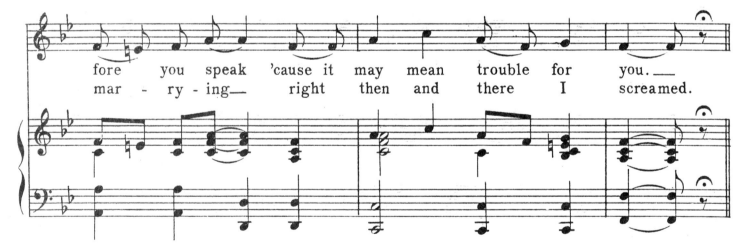

fore you speak 'cause it may mean trouble for you. _____
mar - ry - ing _____ right then and there I screamed.

Chorus.

Take your time _____ friend of mine _____ take your time, _____ Your own time _____
Take your time _____ friend of mine _____ take your time, _____ Your own time _____

p-f

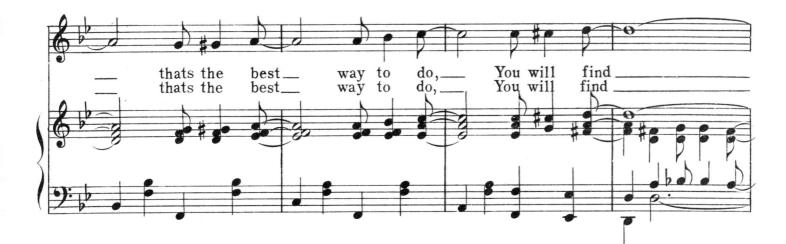

thats the best___ way to do,___ You will find___
thats the best___ way to do,___ You will find___

nev - er let your best friend rush you to trou - bles
when you let take you a wife It's the some as jail for

end, Take your time___ friend of mine___ take your time___
life, Take your time___ sin - gle man___ take your time___

Take your time. ___
Take your time. ___

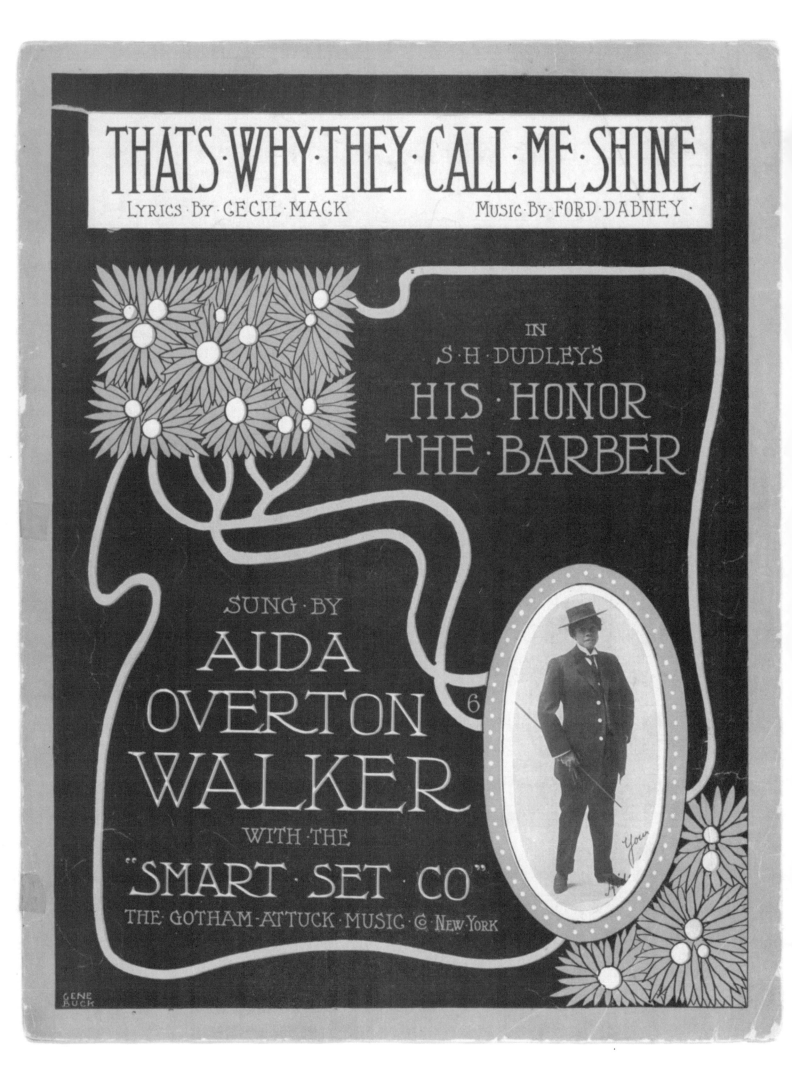

That's Why They Call Me "Shine."

Words by
CECIL MACK

Music by
FORD DABNEY

changed it 'round to Sam-bo, I was Ras-tus to a few _____ Then
ev-'ry thing that's prec-ious from a gold piece to a dime_____ And

Choc'-late drop was add-ed by some oth-ers that I knew, _____ And
dia-monds, pearls and rubies ain't no good un-less they shine, _____ So

then to cap the cli-max I was strolling down the line _____ When
when these clev-er people call me shine or coon or smoke, _____ I

some-one shout-ed "Fel-lers hey, come on and pipe the Shine", _____ But
simp-ly smile then smile some more and vote them all a joke, _____ I'm

in the lat - est style, 'Cause............ I'm glad I'm liv - ing............

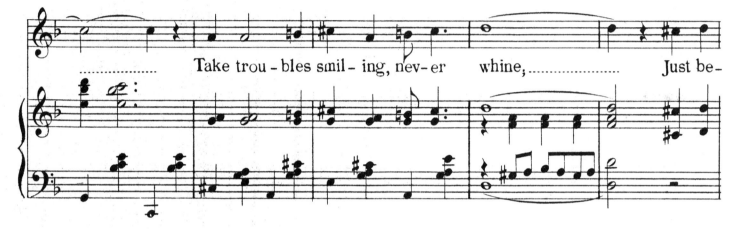

.... Take trou - bles smil - ing, nev - er whine,............ Just be-

cause my color's sha - dy, Slight - ly diff'rent may - be, That's why they

call me "Shine."............ "Shine."............

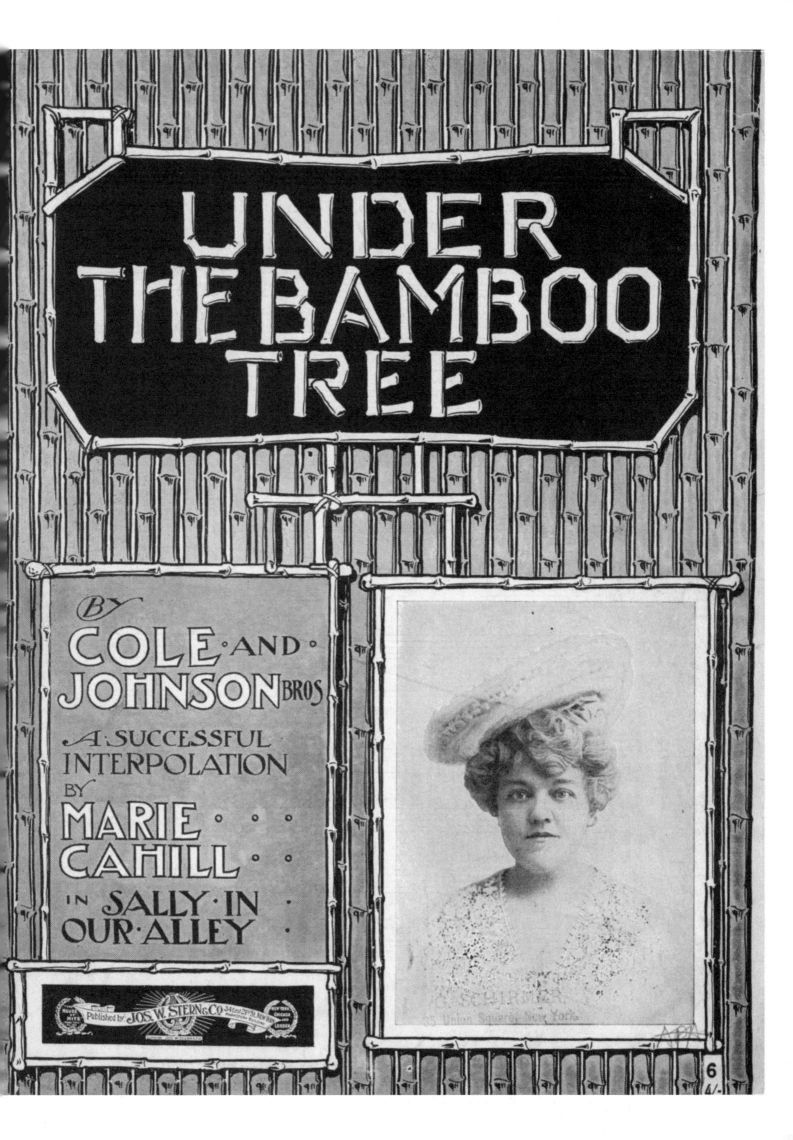

Under The Bamboo Tree.

by BOB COLE.

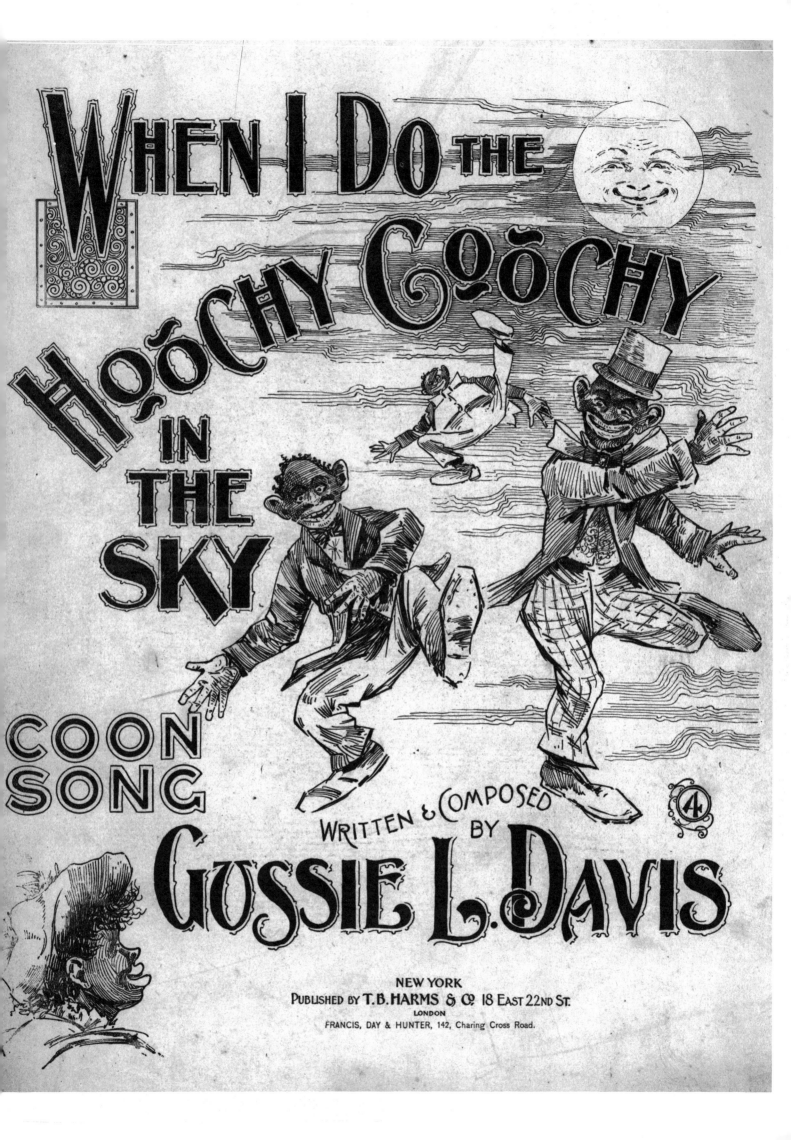

WHEN I DO THE HOOCHY - COOCHY IN DE SKY.

Words & Music by Gussie L. Davis.

1. I aint got no mon-ey and I don't need none, 'Cos I
2. They'll turn the X rays on me when the mu - sic plays, So dat

don't ex - pect to stay here ve - ry long; _____ An'
ev - 'ry - one can see in - to the dance; _____ I'm

raise a big   sen - sa - tion with the white   pop - u - la - tion, When I
lis - ten to   strange ru - mors, but go buy a pair of "bloomers," For to

do   the hoo - chy Coo - chy   in   de   sky!
do   the hoo - chy Coo - chy   in   de   sky!

CHORUS.

When you feel that fun - ny feel-ing, As it   o - ver you is steal-ing, You will

flop your snow-white wings and try to fly;............... I know the

an-gels they will gig-gle When I do that aw-ful wiggle, When I

do the hoo-chy Coo-chy in de sky!".............................

D.C

FAMOUS SONG SUCCESSES IN

COLE & JOHNSON'S

ORIGINAL MUSICAL CREATION

The SHOO-FLY REGIMENT

COLE & JOHNSON

WHO KEEP THE WORLD A-SINGING

BOOK LYRICS & MELODIES BY

COLE & JOHNSON

MANAGEMENT OF

Mr. PHILIP ROBSON

VOCAL

Floating Down The Nile,	60
On The Gay Luneta,	60
Just How Much I Love You,	60
If Adam Had'nt Seen The Apple Tree,	60
There's Always Something Wrong	60
Won't you be my little Brown Bear	60
I'll Die for the Dear Old Flag	60
Sugar Babe	60
Run Brudder Rabbit Run,	60
Ghost Of Deacon Brown,	60
I'll Always Love Old Dixie,	60
Who Do You Love?	60
The Bo'd of Education,	60
Li'l Gal,	60
Old Flag Never Touched The Ground,	60

Published by JOS. W. STERN & CO.

Who do you Love?

Lyric by
BOB COLE

Music by
J. ROSAMOND JOHNSON.